New York Smells

21 postcards and labels for your smelling pleasure

Caroline McKeldin

Photographs by Jay Brady

St. Martin's Paperbacks

Thanks to Bob Biava of Driscoll Labels; Barbara Brackett; Jay Brady; Charlotte Kerr; the wonderful crew at St. Martin's Paperbacks—Roger Cooper, Jennifer Enderlin, Joy Gannon, Matthew Garcia and Amy Kolenik; and my family. Special thanks to Jamie Kershaw for inspiring this book.

NEW YORK SMELLS

Photographs by Jay Brady.

ISBN: 0-312-95632-0

Printed in Mexico

St. Martin's Paperbacks edition/October 1995

10 9 8 7 6 5 4 3 2 1

Fetid New York Harbor

Photo by Jay Brady Photography (1995),
201 E. 62nd St., #3A, New York, NY 10021.
Phone: (212) 371-0158; Fax: (212) 371-0243

Post Card

From *New York Smells.* © 1995 by Caroline McKeldin. St. Martin's Paperbacks.

First
Class
Stamp

**Fulfill your leather fetish in
Greenwich Village**

Post Card

From *New York Smells.* © 1995 by Caroline McKeldin. St. Martin's Paperbacks.

Photo by Jay Brady Photography (1995),
201 E. 62nd St., #3A, New York, NY 10021.
Phone: (212) 371-0158; Fax: (212) 371-0243

**The horse and buggy—
a Central Park tradition**

Post Card

From *New York Smells.* © 1995 by Caroline McKeldin. St. Martin's Paperbacks.

Photo by Jay Brady Photography (1995),
201 E. 62nd St., #3A, New York, NY 10021.
Phone: (212) 371-0158; Fax: (212) 371-0243

A pretzel vendor on every corner...

Post Card

From *New York Smells.* © 1995 by Caroline McKeldin. St. Martin's Paperbacks.

Photo by Jay Brady Photography (1995),
201 E. 62nd St., #3A, New York, NY 10021.
Phone: (212) 371-0158; Fax: (212) 371-0243

**New York taxis—the cheapest
thrill in town**

Post Card

From *New York Smells*. © 1995 by Caroline McKeldin. St. Martin's Paperbacks.

Photo by Jay Brady Photography (1995),
201 E. 62nd St., #3A, New York, NY 10021.
Phone: (212) 371-0158; Fax: (212) 371-0243

**The New York Stock Exchange—where
the smell of money permeates the air**

Post Card

From *New York Smells*. © 1995 by Caroline McKeldin. St. Martin's Paperbacks.

Photo by Jay Brady Photography (1995),
201 E. 62nd St., #3A, New York, NY 10021.
Phone: (212) 371-0158; Fax: (212) 371-0243

Central Park—New York's oasis

Post Card

From *New York Smells*. © 1995 by Caroline McKeldin. St. Martin's Paperbacks.

Photo by Jay Brady Photography (1995),
201 E. 62nd St., #3A, New York, NY 10021.
Phone: (212) 371-0158; Fax: (212) 371-0243

Christmas tree at Rockefeller Center

Post Card

First
Class
Stamp

Photo by Jay Brady Photography (1995),
201 E. 62nd St., #3A, New York, NY 10021.
Phone: (212) 371-0158; Fax: (212) 371-0243

World-famous Katz's Delicatessen —send a salami!

Post Card

From *New York Smells*. © 1995 by Caroline McKeldin. St. Martin's Paperbacks.

Photo by Jay Brady Photography (1995),
201 E. 62nd St., #3A, New York, NY 10021.
Phone: (212) 371-0158; Fax: (212) 371-0243

First
Class
Stamp

Essex Street pickles—Lower East Side

Post Card

From *New York Smells.* © 1995 by Caroline McKeldin. St. Martin's Paperbacks.

Photo by Jay Brady Photography (1995),
201 E. 62nd St., #3A, New York, NY 10021.
Phone: (212) 371-0158; Fax: (212) 371-0243

The hanging ducks of Chinatown

Post Card

From *New York Smells.* © 1995 by Caroline McKeldin. St. Martin's Paperbacks.

Photo by Jay Brady Photography (1995),
201 E. 62nd St., #3A, New York, NY 10021.
Phone: (212) 371-0158; Fax: (212) 371-0243

Fresh at the Fulton Fish Market

Post Card

Photo by Jay Brady Photography (1995),
201 E. 62nd St., #3A, New York, NY 10021.
Phone: (212) 371-0158; Fax: (212) 371-0243

First
Class
Stamp

New York-style pizza

Post Card

From *New York Smells.* © 1995 by Caroline McKeldin. St. Martin's Paperbacks.

Photo by Jay Brady Photography (1995),
201 E. 62nd St., #3A, New York, NY 10021.
Phone: (212) 371-0158; Fax: (212) 371-0243

**New York City: bagel capital
of the world**

Post Card

From *New York Smells.* © 1995 by Caroline McKeldin. St. Martin's Paperbacks.

First
Class
Stamp

Photo by Jay Brady Photography (1995),
201 E. 62nd St., #3A, New York, NY 10021.
Phone: (212) 371-0158; Fax: (212) 371-0243

Garlic wafts through Little Italy

Post Card

First
Class
Stamp

Photo by Jay Brady Photography (1995),
201 E. 62nd St., #3A, New York, NY 10021.
Phone: (212) 371-0158; Fax: (212) 371-0243

Traffic jam in Times Square

Post Card

From *New York Smells.* © 1995 by Caroline McKeldin. St. Martin's Paperbacks.

Photo by Jay Brady Photography (1995),
201 E. 62nd St., #3A, New York, NY 10021.
Phone: (212) 371-0158; Fax: (212) 371-0243

Flowers festoon fashionable Park Avenue

Post Card

First
Class
Stamp

Photo by Jay Brady Photography (1995),
201 E. 62nd St., #3A, New York, NY 10021.
Phone: (212) 371-0158; Fax: (212) 371-0243

**New York, where there's always
a (moldy) place to sleep**

Post Card

From *New York Smells.* © 1995 by Caroline McKeldin. St. Martin's Paperbacks.

First
Class
Stamp

Photo by Jay Brady Photography (1995),
201 E. 62nd St., #3A, New York, NY 10021.
Phone: (212) 371-0158; Fax: (212) 371-0243

St. Patrick's Cathedral

Post Card

First
Class
Stamp

Photo by Jay Brady Photography (1995),
201 E. 62nd St., #3A, New York, NY 10021.
Phone: (212) 371-0158; Fax: (212) 371-0243

Garbage galore in New York City!

Post Card

First
Class
Stamp

Photo by Jay Brady Photography (1995),
201 E. 62nd St., #3A, New York, NY 10021.
Phone: (212) 371-0158; Fax: (212) 371-0243

Subway at rush hour

Post Card

Photo by Jay Brady Photography (1995),
201 E. 62nd St., #3A, New York, NY 10021.
Phone: (212) 371-0158; Fax: (212) 371-0243

First
Class
Stamp

Fetid New York Harbor

Fulfill your leather fetish in Greenwich Village

The horse and buggy—a Central Park tradition

A pretzel vendor on every corner...

New York taxis — the cheapest thrill in town

The New York Stock Exchange

Central Park—New York's oasis

Christmas tree at Rockefeller Center

World-famous Katz's Delicatessen—send a salami!

Essex Street pickles—Lower East Side

The hanging ducks of Chinatown

Fresh at the Fulton Fish Market

New York-style pizza

New York City: bagel capital of the world

Garlic wafts through Little Italy

Traffic jam in Times Square

Flowers festoon fashionable Park Avenue

New York, where there's always a (moldy) place to sleep

St. Patrick's Cathedral

Garbage galore in New York City!

Subway at rush hour